AF477066

This book belongs to:

…………………………………………………………………………………

FLORA

and the

NEW

BABY

Rowena Blyth

Flora met her friends, Buxton and Bear,
at the pond to feed the ducks.
She had something very exciting to tell them!

"My mummy has a baby growing inside her tummy!"
squealed Flora. "I'm going to have a little
brother or sister!"

"That's **BRILLIANT** news!" said Bear.
"I love being a big brother to my little sister."

"Sometimes, when I touch my mummy's tummy,
I can feel the baby move inside," said Flora.

Buxton didn't know anything about babies!
He had lots of questions to ask Flora...

Flora hadn't thought of any of these things
and started to worry.

'Hmmm, maybe I'd quite like things
to stay as they are,' she thought.

"Flora –
you're going
to be a big sister
VERY soon!"
said her mummy,
excitedly.
"Erm, I think
I've changed my mind,"
said Flora. "I've decided
I don't want a baby
brother or sister now.
No thank you, Mummy."

Flora's mummy and daddy explained
that they couldn't send the baby back,
and that being a big sister
would be great fun!

But Flora wasn't so sure.

A week later, the baby arrived,
and Flora went with her daddy to the hospital
to see her mummy and meet the new baby.

"Flora! You've got a little baby brother! And he's bought you a very special present!"
said her mummy, giving Flora a lovely new dolly.

Flora thought the baby
looked a bit red and squashed,
and he was very angry – and noisy!

But, he had given Flora
a really great present.

Later, at Bear's house, Flora was telling
Buxton and Bear all about her new brother.

"All the grown-ups seem to think he's very beautiful
and make such a big fuss about holding him,"
said Flora, confused.

"He's adorable!"
"Can I have a cuddle?"
"Oh, isn't he lovely!"
"Ta-dah!"
"So much so, that they didn't even see me perform my amazing ballet dance show."

"He doesn't really do all that much,"
sighed Flora.

"He doesn't walk...

...or talk...

...or even play with toys!

He sleeps
ALL the
time...

...AND he doesn't even eat
pizza OR ice cream!"
said Flora, looking glum.

"That's because
he's only a little baby,"
said Bear, gently.
"Once he gets a bit bigger,
you'll have lots of
fun together."

At home, Flora's mummy asked her if she
would like to hold her little brother.

"Erm, OK then..." said Flora nervously,
as she sat on the floor and cuddled him.

He felt all warm and squidgy...

...And he was gurgling –
which made Flora giggle!

...Then he smiled back
at Flora and held her finger
with his tiny hand.

"Would you like to help feed him, Flora?"
asked her mummy.

"Erm, OK then..."
said Flora.

As Flora gave her brother his bottle of milk,
he stared up at her with his lovely, big eyes.

'He is **quite** cute, I suppose,'
thought Flora.

Over the next few days,
Flora enjoyed helping with her little brother.

She fetched the cotton wool when
Flora's mummy changed his nappy...

...She played with him
in the bath...

...She helped
get him dressed...

...and gave him his
favourite panda teddy
when he cried.

Flora decided that being a big sister
was quite a lot of fun after all.

Even if he does
wee in the bath!

fourth wall
publishing

First published in Great Britain in 2018 by Fourth Wall Publishing
Copyright © Fourth Wall Publishing 2018
ISBN: 978-1-910851-50-0

www.fourthwallpublishing.com
2 Riverview Business Park, Shore Wood Road, Bromborough, Wirral, Merseyside CH62 3RQ
A catalogue record for this book is available from the British Library
Printed in China